Business Plan

Business Tips How to Start Your Own Business, Make Business Plan and Manage Money (business tools, business concepts, financial freedom, make money easy, money management)

RICK KENNEDY

CONTENTS

I think next books will also be interesting for you:

Leadership Coaching

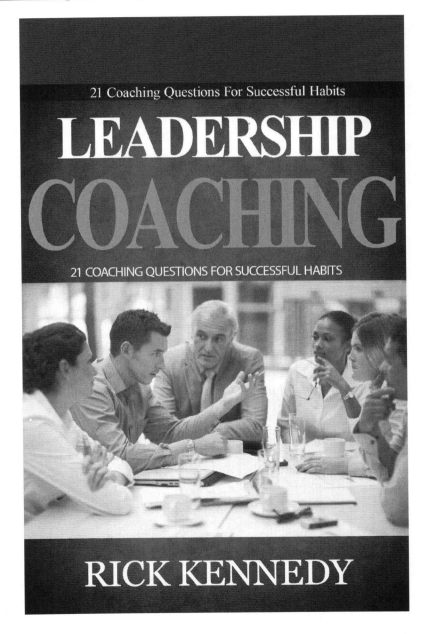

<u>Getting Things Done</u>

How to Organize Your Life

Getting Things Done

Introduction

One of the most fulfilling and rewarding endeavors you can ever embark on is to start and run your own business. Despite the thrills and excitement that come with it, starting and running your business does not come cheap and easy. Starting a business has been likened to starting a family. You need to invest time, dedication and money.

Despite the many challenges associated with running your own business, if you cultivate a strong passion to what you are doing, you will surely be successful.

I must also add that passion alone is not enough. You need to equip yourself with the necessary information that may be required to run the business you intend going into. With a strong passion, your willingness to learn, coupled with a strong urge to apply what you learn, you are surely on your way to becoming one of the most successful business owners. The trick is to start small and gather momentum along the way. This will give you the needed confidence to take on larger responsibilities and projects.

Chapter 1: Your Decision and Motivation to Start a Business

If you have this book in your possession, it communicates one major thing: you have decided to get out of the rat race and establish your own profitable business. I must commend you for this bold decision. I must also add that your decision to start your own business is not sufficient to carry you through the rough times that many entrepreneurs go through. The road to entrepreneurship is mainly that of moving out of the crowd and making an impact for yourself and family. Most people won't dare leave their comfort zones and establish something they would be proud of.

Mostly when you are growing your business, there are times you may go without any incomes coming in. Your suppliers may disappoint you. Your clients might opt for different products or services. Your advertising campaigns might not always work as you expect. These and many other reasons make the route to entrepreneurship very challenging and burdensome. You therefore need to be highly convinced and be sure that this is what you want to do. Your motivation will go a long way to help you remain strong even in difficult times.

You also need to firmly establish that you've got what it takes to go on your own and run a business. Conduct an objective assessment of your strengths and weaknesses. Ask yourself these probing questions, which I call my 11-point test:

1. Are you motivated and self-confident enough?
2. Are you strong-minded and determined?
3. Do you have a positive outlook to life?
4. Are you trainable and willing to take on professional advice?
5. Can you accept challenges and learn from them?
6. Do you have detailed technical knowledge about your proposed business?
7. Are you physically, emotionally and mentally sound enough to run a business?
8. Do you have the endurance to put in longer hours, just to make sure your business operates properly?
9. Can you sell a product or service, as well as market yourself?
10. Do you have a thorough knowledge of the market you intend to enter?
11. How good are you at analyzing problems and coming up with workable solutions?

Congratulations if you answered "yes" to 75 per cent of the questions. You are fit to start your own business. If you passed the 11-point test, then I must say that you stand to gain a lot by starting your business. Here are some benefits you stand to gain when you are running your own business:

- Running your business can be financially rewarding. You generate your own incomes and profits. I am yet to meet anyone who has truly been wealthy by working for another person. The possibilities for making money whilst running a business are limitless. You are absolutely in charge of what strategies to employ so you generate the needed incomes and profits.
- You have the freedom to do what you really enjoy and manage successfully. This is because you take decisions you are very convinced would help the business grow.
- Your creativity is well exhibited when you run your own business.
- You become your own boss, determining deciding what to do without taking orders from anyone.
- You determine your own working hours. You may put in more or less hours, depending on how well you want to grow the business.
- You take complete charge of what happens to you, without the constant fear of being laid off.
- If you happen to employ people, you put smiles on their faces and that of their families as well.
- You are very fulfilled, knowing that you are pursuing your passion.

Chapter 2: Testing Your Business Idea

You may have a very brilliant business idea that you are so much passionate about. I must caution that a brilliant idea is not the same as a viable idea. The purpose of a business is to generate enough money and be profitable. Without money coming in, the fortunes of your business would quickly dwindle and the business will eventually phase out. If the business you intend to operate won't be viable, a lot of your scarce resources would just be washed down the drain. Your energy will also be wasted. You will sooner or later be frustrated and give up trying to run that business. To ensure that you don't waste your efforts and resources, you need to subject your business idea to a test, to establish its viability.

Get enough data about your potential clients. What are the demographics of your clients? What age range do they fall into? What are their tastes and preferences? As part of idea testing, you also need to have information about your competitors. What kinds of products and services are they offering? At what quality and prices are they being offered? Is your proposed product or service going to offer value that distinguishes it from the competition? What will make people decide to purchase what you have to offer?

Finding answers to these relevant questions will go a long way to ensure your business has a higher probability of succeeding on the market. Typical sources of information about your clients and market include government statistical data, business reports and the local chamber of commerce. Subscribing to, and reading business news also presents very current information about market trends.

The internet is an important source of information, which can feed your business with data about your potential clients and market. You however need to filter the information available to you and use what will be needed.

Chapter 3: Preparing Your Business Plan

Once you've tested your business idea to ascertain its viability, you need to prepare a business plan. A business plan outlines the key and functional areas of your business such as operations, management, finance and marketing. The business plan serves as a roadmap for your business. A business plan assists you, the entrepreneur to plan and expand the business. The business plan also information to potential investors and lenders about the feasibility and profitability of the business. Without a business plan, nobody is going to take you seriously and offer any support they may have.

The plan can serve as internal document for the use of management or as guide to identify quality employees and potential partners. The plan may be termed as a feasibility document because it identifies the strengths, weaknesses, opportunities and threats (SWOT) of the business. The plan can also assist in management decision making and serve as a guide to monitoring and evaluation of your operations.

The key elements of a business plan are covered below.

1. Cover Page and Executive Summary

On the cover page, you need to clearly state the name of the business and contact information (addresses, phone numbers and e-mail addresses). Also, you need to include the date on which the plan was created. The date helps you to keep track when revisions to the plan are made in future. The Executive Summary, which is usually the last to be written, gives a glimpse of the major issues in the plan. Though it is recommended that it should not be more than one page, it is expected to generate enough interest in your readers to urge them to read the entire document.

2. The Industry, the Company and its Products

The product or a service you intend to introduce is situated in a particular industry. You therefore need to describe your business in the context of that industry. You need to come up with enough reasons for introducing the product or service. Also, state the company's legal structure, its mission and vision. The mission of your business must communicate the main reason for its existence. The vision is where you intend to take the business in the foreseeable years. A strong vision drives the operations of the business. Give a detailed description of the product or services. Important information you need to include are:

- The benefits your potential clients stand to gain by patronizing your services.
- Intended quality level and use
- Proposed price
- Technical developments involved
- Regulatory status such as environmental requirements
- For services, think about how you intend addressing issues of warranties, marketing and technical support.

3. Market and Research Analysis

For your marketing efforts to be successful, you need access to relevant and updated information. Market and research analysis requires that you conduct an objective assessment of who your competitors are and the products or services they offer. What would differentiate your products or services from what they are offering already? Finding and answer to this question gives you products or services a competitive advantage over others on the market. Establish persuasive reasons why clients would rather choose to purchase what you are offering. Factors such as pricing, quality and prompt response to customer complaints may distinguish your products or services from those on the market.

4. Marketing Plan

Your success as an entrepreneur depends on having a solid customer base. Without customers to patronize your products or services, you are out of business. In your marketing plan, you need to give detailed procedures for attracting and retaining your customers. Your marketing plan needs to be in place, as long as your business is in operation. In your marking plan, include the following:

- Overall market strategy
- Pricing and sales tactics
- Advertising and promotion
- Packaging

A marketing plan must clearly define the market, marketing trends, your market share, methods you can use to increase your share and how you can increase your profitability.

You must note that marketing and planning is an on-going process. You therefore need to put in measures to do some periodic evaluations to ensure your plans are achieving their intended outcomes. You need to do this for your business to keep pace with the ever evolving and changing customer preferences.

5. Operating Plan

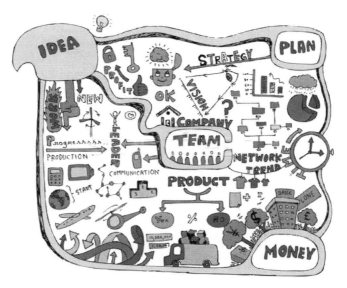

In your operating plan, state issues that are critical to the business operations and give you a competitive advantage. Your operating plan therefore covers areas such as labor, materials, facilities, equipment and processes. When you are in a service industry, your operating plan is quite different from a manufacturing industry. You would normally have higher labor requirement and lower investments in manufacturing plants and equipment.

If you intend going into manufacturing, you need to know where you can reliably source materials for production. You also need to know the backgrounds and track records of your suppliers, to be sure they can meet your demands. As a back-up, you may need to establish relationships with other suppliers in case your regular suppliers have a challenge with getting you materials.

For both the service and manufacturing industry, you need very competent staff to man various sections of your operations.

6. Management Team

This part lists the management team and their backgrounds. Also, include the structure, duties and responsibilities, management compensation and ownership. Within your management team, include a list of business advisors and a board of directors. This may be formal or informal, based on the scale of the business. The key point to note is to include people who have vast industry experience and can deliver value to your business.

If you are managing your business alone, it's equally important to describe your background in relation to type of business you intend operating. A competent and an experienced management team give potential investors and lenders the confidence that the business would be handled competently and become profitable.

7. Financial Plan

Developing a financial plan is a specialized skill which you definitely need the help of an accountant, counselor or an accomplished business person to finish. You need to do this if you don't have an accounting background. The financial plan basically consists of a five-year plan with forecasts to justify your estimates. The financial plan generally consists of four parts. These are:

a)   List of requirements, sources of information and reserves.

b)   Description of your financial plan and all sources of capital.

c)   Beginning balance sheet

d)   Complete statement of projected operations and cash flows.

When you are preparing the business plan, you need to take note of the following:

- Avoid too much detail that is not essential to the plan. Also, don't make it to snappy such that vital information is lost.

- The graphics you use should complement the substance in the plan but not as a substitute for logic and reasoning.

- There should be an executive summary because some of your readers only have just enough time to go through the executive summary.

- The plan should be written in clear and understandable language, without any technical jargons.

- As the business owner, anticipate possible problems that may arise whilst implementing the plan and put in contingency measures to address them.

- Don't forget to come up with a strong marketing plan. Cash flow in a business is what accounts for the existence of the business, and marketing brings in the needed incomes.

- You should show enough commitment and passion towards your business. You need to prove that you are willing to invest your own resources into the business. This would ensure that other people will also be convinced enough to invest in the business.

Chapter 4: Determining the Type Of Business Structure You Want To Operate

Determining the type of business entity you want to operate is very critical because this decision has serious legal, financial and other implications. The main forms of business structures are sole proprietorship, partnership, Limited Liability Company, and franchises.

The sole proprietorship is the simplest form of business. This is a one-person managed business. You don't need any special legal steps to begin. Accounting and tax operations are also the simplest. You and your business are considered the same.

As a sole proprietor, you may or may not give your business a name. The profits you make off your business are considered your salary. If you happen to accumulate any debts, your personal money or your properties will be used to defray the debt.

Another business structure is the partnership. The level of regulation in partnership is quite low. Before you decide to form a partnership, you should think carefully about what the other party would be contributing to the business.

The contribution of your partner could be in the form of financial resources, a special skill or valuable network. The advantage in a partnership lies in the fact that the resources and skills of two or more people are pulled and used in the business. The downside to partnership is that when one partner leaves, the partnership is dissolved.

As the name implies, a limited liability company provides limited liability for the owners. The owners of a limited liability company risk only their investment in the event that the business fails. In other words, their personal funds are not part of the business. They are therefore not held personally liable for any debts which the company incurs.

If you want to operate your business as a franchise, you run it with a product or service that has already gained success on the market. You can operate a franchise as a sole proprietor, partnership or limited liability. In a franchise, you operate your business entirely using the name of a successful company. Before you decide to run a franchise, talk to some of the company's existing franchises, check the franchisor's management structure and examine their history. All these checks are necessary to ensure that your business does not fail.

A snapshot of the advantages and disadvantages of the various types of business structures are provided below:

Business structure	Pros	Cons
Sole Proprietorship	It can easily be set up You have complete control over the business	You are personally liable for all your debts You have no access to equity capital, which is relatively risk-free
Partnership	You share risk and investment You have a wider pool	You share profits You are liable for all debts. You will need a carefully drafted

	of skills and resources	partnership agreement, which is quite expensive
Limited Liability Company	You are not personally liable for debts The business image is better projected	More complex to set up. You will need more professional advice, which is usually expensive
Franchise	You will usually need less money than would have been needed to set up a similar business. You can rely on the support, brands and reputation of a household name.	The franchisor has a fair degree of control over your business You have to pay the franchisor some royalties.

Now that you have an appreciable knowledge of the types of business structures and the various advantages and disadvantages associated with them, it is very important to choose a business that serves your best interest and ensures that it generates enough profits for you and your and your team. Do an objective assessment of your personal strengths and weaknesses and make a firm decision to use one.

Chapter 5: Financing Your Business

We can't dispute the fact that we need money to run our businesses. However you need to answer some pertinent questions before you embark on a drive to raise money for your business. Do you know all the sources of potential finance? How much do you need exactly? When will you need the money? Think about how much you need for the business to run before it generates income. Sometimes you may not need all the money at a go, so staggering it will save you a lot of interest repayment. You will also need to state what the money will be used for. When you are able to provide a convincing answer, you stand a high chance of getting the money from your bankers and potential investors. They just want to make sure the business will generate enough money so you can pay off your debt.

As a potential business owner, you need to do due diligence by researching the various sources of finance available. Your aim should be to access the most cost-effective means of financing your business.

Typical sources of money for your business include:

- Your personal money: If you are really desirous of starting a business, you need to commit some of your own money into it. Whilst this may not be much, it gives an impression to outside investors and lenders that your investment in the business goes beyond your labor.

- Family and friends: There is little or no paperwork or legal issues associated with sourcing money from family and friends. With this source of finance, you need to be faithful and communicate any challenges you may have that would affect your ability to pay the money as agreed. Money issues can ruin an otherwise cordial relationship with your family and friends.

- Bank loan: Banks provide short-, mid-, or long-term financing for businesses. They finance various asset needs such as working capital and procurement of equipment. Some banks will require guarantees or collaterals in the form of your assets and other landed properties.

In exceptional cases, you can use a well crafted business plan to secure a loan with some banks. Despite signing an agreement with a bank to finish the repayment of loan within a stipulated time, you can as well finish paying off the loan earlier when you have the money in bulk. This offers an advantage in the sense that the total interest paid would be reduced.

- Government and non-governmental economic development agencies: There are various interventions by the state and other non-governmental agencies to help budding entrepreneurs and business owners. There are budgetary allocations that are targeted at financing businesses on an annual basis.

You need to find out from your state or other trade and commerce institutions to know the requirements for accessing the funds. The competition for assistance may be high but you stand a higher chance of getting help if you follow the various modalities they have put in place. Also, you stand a higher chance of getting funding if your proposed business intends to generate positive social outcomes.

Customers: When your business is up and running, you may be able to secure some advance payment from your customers in anticipation that you will deliver a certain service or some quantities of products. When customers are able to give you advance payment, they are convinced that you can deliver value to them. You therefore need to fulfill your part of the bargain by delivering the required quality and quantity to them.

Chapter 6: Marketing and Selling

An effective promotional strategy for your business goes a long way to attract clients. One basic marketing model that has been proven to work for several years is the 4Ps of marketing mix-product, price, place and promotion. To get a better understanding of the marketing mix, answer the following questions:

- How will your clients benefit from your product or service?

- How important will the price be to them?

- Where will the product be sold?

- How will the product be promoted?

Now let's tackle each of the four elements of the marketing mix.

1. Product

 Think about what value the product or service will deliver to your clients. You can do this by looking at the features of the product. Come up with a list of the qualities of your product or service which will appeal to your customers. Now for each product feature, write next to it the benefit the customer intends to get. Spend some time to think about what clients look for in products and services of that nature.

2. Price

To better price your product or service, list your competitors' products and their prices. How do their prices compare with yours? Remember you don't need to lower your prices to attract clients, if indeed you are offering a product of superior value and quality. What are the characteristics of your clients? Are they low-income, middle-income or high-income earners? Finding answers to these would give you an indication as to whether your clients have money to spend on the product or service you are offering.

Another side of looking at the competition is that other unrelated products are also competing for the money of your customer. For instance, if you are a car retailer, your competitors may not necessarily be other car dealers. The consumer may be torn between the choice of buying a new car and moving into a bigger apartment.

The price you set for your product must deliver a profit margin to you. You need to factor all the operational costs and other expenses which may not be so glaring. Also, think about what would come into your customer's mind when they think of your business. What image are you portraying? Is it budget, luxury or premium?

There are various reasons why customers would want to purchase a particular product or service. There are some clients who will not mind spending some extra money, for the pride of being known to use a certain product or service. For such clients, price may not be an important consideration in their purchase decision.

Place

You should think about a "place" where your products or services will be sold. With the advent of modern communication tools, a physical location is becoming less relevant. There are companies that have annual turnovers in billions of dollars, yet they don't have any physical location. All their transactions are done online, through the medium of the internet. Other "places" you that are available are door-to-door, direct mail or wholesaling. New marketing dynamics suggest that you don't really need a physical location to be able to sell your product or service. The most important thing is to remember that wherever you choose to sell your product, it must deliver value and convenience to your clients.

3. Promotion

In promoting your business, you aim to tell your potential customers that you exist. Promotion also seeks to explain the benefits of your products to clients. In promoting your business, you convince your potential clients that you are delivering something of much better value than what is already available. Your ultimate aim will be to turn your clients into repeated buyers who will remain loyal and also recommend your business to others.

Aside the various promotional vehicles to consider, you need to carefully draft a convincing and persuasive message. Get value for your money by using the most appropriate media to carry your messages. Various promotional mediums you can use include:

- TV advertising

- Newspaper and magazine advertising

- Door-to –door leafleting

- Use of Yellow Pages

- Billboard posters

These days it's not uncommon to see most businesses having an online presence, through the use of websites or other social media platforms. For authors, Amazon has become a preferred platform to promote their works. If you intend having an online presence for your business, you have to put in a lot of effort to make sure you get people visiting your page. Regularly update your page to reflect a current listing of products and services you have on offer. Being responsive to customer queries and complaints will certainly distinguish you from your competitors. If you shop around, you can get a good deal on fees charged for hosting your website. You can also get many website templates to use. All you need is to input your information.

Chapter 7: Controlling Your Business

Once your business is up and running, you need to put in systems of control that would ensure that your business stays on track. Without any control measures, you would probably mistake the cash coming in for the profits. If this continues, the business will surely head in a downward spiral.

Setting up financial controls constitutes an essential element in the overall control system. Your financial records and book-keeping must be up –to- date. For an effective financial control, you must know:

- Your exact financial situation.

- Your forecast position for the months ahead.

- The position required to meet your budgets.

- Any mitigation measures to address financial challenges

- The effectiveness of your actions with respect to reviewing the performance of your business.

The above can be known only when you have good financial records available. If you are too busy to compile the financial records, you can delegate this duty to someone who is competent. You however need to monitor to ensure the right thing is being done.

Another form of control is for you to understand the tax system. A firm knowledge of the tax system can work in your favor. There are various tax rebates and incentives you can take advantage of, as a business person. You need to check with your state revenue authority.

Conclusion

I am confident this book has given you the needed stimulus to begin thinking of starting your own business, if you have not yet made that firm decision. Running your business presents some challenges. This should not however stop you from pursuing something you are really passionate about.

If you have access to quality information such as that contained in this book, your walk down the often lonely path of entrepreneurship would eventually present huge benefits. The journey to set up and run your own profitable business is one of the most rewarding and fulfilling ventures you can undertake. Running your own business is also a route to financial freedom and wealth creation.

I therefore encourage you to take the necessary steps to implement the valuable pieces of advice this book presents, and your journey towards setting up your own business will be much smoother. If you are already running your business, use this book as a source of reference and your business will definitely move to a higher level.

A Beginners Guide to Master Simple Sales Techniques and Increase Sales

SALES

A Beginners Guide to Master Simple Sales Techniques and Increase Sales

DANIEL R. COVEY

Sales

A Beginners Guide to Master Simple Sales Techniques and Increase Sales (sales, best tips, sales tools, sales strategy, close the deal, business development, influence people, cold calling)

DANIEL R.COVEY

CONTENTS

Introduction

The foundation of every business is sales, for without selling anything, businesses would not survive the tough markets that they are in today. It is important then, for businesses and individuals alike, to then learn all of the necessary skills to be successful in sales and then keep learning as the market constantly changes and evolves.

However, the sales industry is much more than being about sales – it must be about your customers, and more specifically, the needs of your customers. In order to understand these needs you must be asking questions to identify these needs – for if you do not ask what it is that your customer actually wants, then how will you possibly know what it is that they want?

For that reason, to be successful in the sales industry, you must change your focus from making sales to making relationships. Businesses are built on repeat business and customers buy things from the people that they trust, so this should be your focus.

This book is a beginners guide to mastering simple sales techniques in order to increase sales, and will cover all of the necessary factors which are required in order to achieve this. You will learn everything from how to develop relationships, to overcoming customer objections, and the latest tools and sales strategies of which you can use on your journey to becoming a successful salesperson.

Chapter 1 – What is Sales?

In the recent movie *The Wolf of Wall Street*, directed my Martin Scorsese, there is a scene in which the protagonist, Jordan Belfort (played by Leonardo DiCaprio), asks his friends to "Sell me this pen". Most of his friends start by saying how appealing or attractive this pen would be to Jordan, thinking that the key to sales is to pitch to the customer the products features and attributes. However, one of the friends, Brad, immediately grabs then pen and asks Jordan to write something down for him. Jordan replies that he does not have a pen to do so, and thus the sale is made. This is the definition of sales. The character Brad realizes what Jordan is asking him to do. He is not really asking his friends to sell him the pen, rather he is asking them to realize that sales is all about the needs of the buyer. People are not going to buy what they do not need or what they do not want – they will only buy what is of immediate value to them.

There is a saying which says "No one buys what you sell, they only buy what is of value to them". This basically means that you should not be selling the marketing of a product (its features and benefits), but rather you should be selling your product as an actual solution to fill your customers needs. In the *Wolf of Wall Street* example above, Brad has recognized that Jordan does not have a pen, so he is able to fill the need of selling Jordan a pen the moment he actually needs a pen. The customer has gone from not valuing the pen one moment (by listening to all the various features and benefits of the pen), to valuing it strong enough the next moment that he needs to buy it. If you are able to recognize the needs of your customers as well as this example, you will go very far as a professional salesperson.

HOW DOES SALES DIFFER FROM MARKETING?

The most effective salespeople in business today don't want their customers to buy *from* them, but rather they want their customers to build a relationship *with* them. The key to a successful sales business is repeat business. This relationship should ultimately be built on trust, and even though there are some very crafty salespeople out there who can get people to even buy what they do not need, this dishonesty and greed will eventually bring any business down, as customers only buy from people of whom they trust. Just as much as you are trying to build customers for life, if they find out that you have been lying to them, you will lose those customers for life.

The biggest difference between sales and marketing is that although both lead to sales, marketing tends to be more about features and benefits to a wide audience at once, whereas sales is generally a personalized and tailored one-on-one experience. Marketing tells stories to the customer, and sales is where those stories become real for the customer. Marketing also looks after the brands reputation, whereas sales looks after individuals. As you can see, although marketing and sales seem very similar in nature, and essentially work towards the same goal in the business world, they are defined in two completely different ways. So make sure that you know the difference when applying them to your business or personal career.

WHAT TRAITS DO SUCCESSFUL SALESPEOPLE HAVE?

Every person who is in the sales business will approach their sales methods in different ways. For example, one sales person might offer each of his customers a coffee, whereas another salesperson might simply wear a suit and tie and be neat and presentable at all times. However, apart from their methods, every successful salesperson shares five traits: discipline, tenacity, implementation, focus and desire. Some salespeople might have more focus than desire, and some salespeople might have more tenacity than implementation, but what is important here is understanding that if you are able to develop each of these five traits, then you will become a very successful salesperson.

DISCIPLINE

The definition of discipline is to create daily habits that you stick to doing and achieving every single day. Discipline and habits can be considered the same thing, for as we discipline ourselves to do things, over time these will become habits that we will not even have to think about doing for them to get done. When was the last time that you had to think about brushing your teeth before bed? Develop this level of discipline in relation to the sales tools needed to succeed, and you will surely succeed.

TENACITY

Tenacity means the quality or fact of being able to grip something firmly or relentlessly. In other words, an all-or-nothing attitude. To apply this to a salesperson, to be successful you must give your customers and business your complete attention at all times. Remember, that at the root of any sales process is the exchange of or potential of money, so don't let an opportunity pass you just because you couldn't be bothered to remain engaged or give the potential sale 100% of your attention.

IMPLEMENTATION

Implementation is probably one of the most important traits that a successful salesperson can have. To implement something basically means to put into action what you have learned. In other words, you should implement or put into practice the key tools and strategies that you are learning whilst reading this book. Also make it a good habit to not give yourself the excuse that you are not smart enough to do something, or don't have the right tools to succeed – just remember that it is up to you to learn new things and then to apply those in your life, business and career.

FOCUS

Focus means to hold your attention strongly and completely on a goal that you wish strongly to achieve. It also means not allowing distractions to get in the way between you and those goals, or other people distracting you by telling you that you are not good enough or not better than them. It will be good practice for you to practice the art of concentration so that you can create for yourself powerful focus for anything that you want in life. See if you can count to 100 without thinking about anything else other than counting. If you start thinking about other things or forget what number you were up to, start from one again until you can reach 100 without being distracted. This is the level of focus that you should learn to cultivate.

DESIRE

You must want your goals and success as much as you want to breathe after holding your breath for a minute. Desire is the ultimate trait out of these five, because if you don't want something then you are not going to do anything about trying to reach it. Just make sure that you remain realistic and understand that success does not happen overnight. It will take some time, so work on developing these five traits every day, and before you know it, you will be a very successful salesperson.

Chapter 2 – How to Close the Sale

Once we have identified what the customer needs, as explained at the start of Chapter One, we can then work on actually making the sale by giving the customer what they need. However, sometimes it takes a little bit more work than asking the question "do you want to buy this product", because you may find that the customer will feel pressured and say no. It's funny, because even though we have exactly what the customer wants, there is something deep within the human psyche that still wants to push back and reject any offer of salvation. As a guide, instead of asking for the purchase, why not try asking the following question instead.

"If I gave you the product at this low price, would there be any reason why you would not want to buy it today?"

This suddenly makes the customer realize that they are going to have to say more than "yes" or "no", although if the customer does say "no" then you have effectively made the sale. However, if the customer says that there is a reason why they do not want to product today, then you can ask further questions to find out what is holding them back. Perhaps the price is out of their budget range, or maybe they wanted a different color or style of the product that you are offering them.

Asking quality questions is the most important first step of the sales process. If we ask customers what they want, we will know what they want. Sometimes we may have to ask different questions to get the need out of them, such as *"What can I do today that is going to help you the most?"*, because if we just ask for the sale without understanding exactly what it is that the customer wants, then they will see right through us. Remember that successful salespeople and sales businesses are built on trust and relationships. If we see the customer's merely as dollar signs rather than human beings with feelings and needs, then we will not go very far at all in the sales business. This is why you should always be having conversations with your customers instead of merely asking them straight away if they want to buy your products.

Chapter 3 – Sales Tools

When most people think about the tools that they can use in their sales business or sales career, they immediately think about CRM (Customer Relationship Management) software such as SalesForce.com, or networking social media websites such as LinkedIn.

It is important to understand that humans have been using

tools for thousands of years, from the prehistoric to the modern man – so too have the tools of technology have evolved and are now today quite incredibly advanced. Just think about what we can do on our phones today that we could not do even 5 years ago.

The same rule applies to the tools within the sales industry. Unlike the sales professionals of days gone past, sales are no longer done exclusively with a telephone directory and a headset. Here are nine sales tools that you should consider should you want to be ahead of your competition.

YESWARE and SIGNALS

Most communication between businesses and customers these days is done through email. But we all should know the pain of sending an email and waiting for a reply, always asking ourselves "have they even opened the email yet?". Luckily both of these tools can help. Yesware and Signals work by alerting us as soon as our customer opens their email and reads it. This provides the perfect opportunity to call them. Imagine how highly they will think of you if they have just finished reading your prospectus and then you call.

BOOMERANG

There are certain times of the day that are considered to be the best time to send somebody an email that they will actually read – the earlier the better as the old saying goes. People are more likely to read a new email whilst they are reading their inbox, which normally occurs in the period between 8:30 and 9am. However, what if you are scheduled for a meeting then? Luckily with this tool, you can schedule certain times for emails to be sent that you have pre-written, making sure that you never miss out on the golden hour of opportunity.

LINKEDIN and other SOCIAL MEDIA

Most people regard LinkedIn as only a social media platform to look for work or employment. However, this is not the case anymore, and innovative sales professionals at the head of the game have realized that LinkedIn and other social media platforms (such as Facebook, Twitter and Google+) are perfect for finding new prospects to sell to. Join groups within your target market, and start doing your research to dish out those sales.

GOOGLE ALERTS

Google Alerts is a very powerful tool, in that it does all of your social media browsing for you. No longer do you have to go through each of the pages of your social media platforms to read the latest updates from your friends, groups and followers. This tool will alert you each time one of these people posts a new update, meaning that you will have access to the latest news, even before your competition if they do not have this tool. This is how you stay ahead in the sales business.

RAPPORTIVE

Rapportive is a free sales tool which will link together your LinkedIn and Gmail accounts, so that when we are emailing our client or prospect, we will see a brief summary of their LinkedIn account on the side so not only do we know who we are emailing (especially if emailing a lot of people every day), but also so that we are able to build strong rapport and relationships with these people by commenting on their latest update for example. Remember that relationships are key to a successful sales business or career.

SALES LOFT

Sales Loft will save you hundreds of hours of work by importing all of your social media contacts into one database, complete with email addresses and phone numbers, which then can be used as a contact directory, or even for your next marketing and sales campaign.

DOCURATED

Docurated helps you create customized content for your prospects quickly and easily. This will allow you to locate specific keywords which relate directly to the individual or business which you are targeting, and then create relevant presentations for you based on those keywords. Your customers will see that you have put the time and effort into creating a presentation that is personal and unique specifically for them.

DATANYZE

This is a wonderful tool which will allow your sales representatives, or even yourself, the ability to track the customers that are buying from your competition, and more importantly, which customers have stopped buying from them. These customers would be other businesses that are within your target market, so if this tool tells you that a contract has just ended between them and your competitor, pick up the phone straight away and get them on board. Make sure that you find out why they left so that you can be sure that you do not make the same mistake.

TINDERBOX

TinderBox is perfect in the sales cycle when you are closing the sale. The tool will automatically create for you contracts, documents, emails, electronic signatures and so forth to make sure that the end of the sales cycle with your customers is as smooth and efficient as possible. The tool will also keep all of the information in your CRM software up-to-date, meaning that you will never be caught out giving your customers incorrect or out-dated information.

As you can see, the advance of technology has opened up the potential to allow businesses and individuals alike in the sales industry access to these tools which will revolutionize the way that they interact with customers. Put these tools in your hands or in the hands of your sales representatives, and watch your sales figures skyrocket.

Chapter 4 – How to Influence People

In order to be successful in sales, you must learn how to be a great leader. Anyone can be a leader, but true leadership comes from the deep innate ability or skill which allows you to influence people. If you look back through the pages of history, strong and influential people have ruled armies which had build dynasties and toppled kingdoms - although our sales business should not be managed to that extreme. The first step that you should take is to believe in yourself.

The biggest obstacle in doing this is that we as humans have the uncanny ability to constantly doubt ourselves. Thinking that we do not have what it takes to be the best that we want to be, we give in to fear and hinder our abilities before we even start. Realize that our biggest enemies are ourselves.

However, the most successful people that we see around us do not give in to this state of mind. They apply the five traits of successful people and overcome this silly obstacle, and then they are able to continue working on developing the skills required to influence people. The question is how do we influence people? When you think about it, it really comes down to leading by example – that kind of leadership that you share with your closest friends and family members. So, the question should rather be, how do you make more friends?

Making more friends definitely sounds better than the phrase "winning" more friends. So, how can this be achieved? What is it that we do that makes friends for us? It really comes down to five skills of which we should apply to every conversation that we have with people – sales prospects or strangers on the street.

1. Give your complete attention to someone else and show genuine interest in everything that they say to you.

2. Make sure that you do not forget their name (write it down if possible, or get a business card).

3. Listen to every word that they say.

4. Make the person feel important – that they are in the center of your attention.

5. Smile and thank them for their time.

When you think about it, isn't this the way that we act around our close friends and family members? This is how you should be acting around every person that you meet. Remember that the secret to a successful sales business is to build relationships to form long-term customers who will buy from you many times, so if we are able to master the art of relationship building, we should be able to turn every person that we meet into a loyal customer for life.

Chapter 5 – Sales Strategy

Just as the way as we are developing our decisions in the way that we interact and develop relationships with our customers, so too are they developing the way that they make decisions about how and why they purchase. These decision-making processes are constantly changing, so it is important to continually re-evaluate the way that you go about selling your products and services to your customers. You must also remember the difference between sales and marketing, and make sure that when you are selling, you do not come across as arrogant or as if you are not paying attention to what the customer has said in relation to what they actually need from you.

In essence, a sales strategy consists of a plan which positions a company's brand or product in order to gain a competitive advantage. The most successful types of sales strategies assist your sales team in focusing on target market customers and helping them communicate with them in helpful, relevant, and meaningful ways. Your sales representatives, and yourself, need to know how your products and/or services can be used to solve your customers problems. To be successful, your sales strategy should always be focused on presenting to the customers within your target market, else you will be wasting time trying to sell to customers who you have not tailored your products for.

In saying this, you should be well aware by now that in the sales business, your customer's needs should always come first. You should be asking as many relevant and quality questions as possible to make sure that what you are offering your customer is actually what they need. Sales is built on trust, and repeat business is the foundation of long-term success in the sales industry (or for any business for that matter), so lets have a look at six of the most effective steps that you can implement today to help you make sales and close the deal more efficiently.

IDENTIFY WHO MAKES THE BUYING DECISIONS

It is quite obvious when selling, that the only person who will buy or has the authority to buy, is the decision-maker. This especially applies when you are trying to win over a business as a new customer. You should always do your research first and try and understand how the decision-maker makes decisions, what motivates them to buy, and so on. Always customize and personalize your sales pitch so that you are specifically targeting that customer, and only that customer, at that time.

BE REALISTIC

When tailoring your sales pitch for the customer, make sure that you do not come across as too calculated, as this can actually scare some people off. In other words, show the customer that you care about identifying their needs and providing a solution to fix those needs rather than just making a quick sale. Remember that honesty and relationship-building are keys to success in the sales industry.

CREATE URGENCY

Your goal as a successful salesperson, is to get the customer to buy right now. You can't let your customer walk out of the door and say that they will be back next week, because they will either never come back, or they will buy from somebody else (you competition!). Whether you use your skills of persuasion by asking questions, or offer a discount if they purchase right now, or simply inform them that this price is only valid for today – when they come back next week, the product will be more expensive.

DEALING WITH OBJECTIONS

As discussed in Chapter Two, we need to ask for the sale in a way that if the customer is going to say no, that they are obligated to say more than no. Remember, ***"If I gave you the product at this low price, would there be any reason why you would not want to buy it today?"***. This sentence should be used at the end of every single one of your sales pitches. Not every customer, no matter how hard we try, is going to buy from us. But, we need to make sure that we understand and ask the reasons for them not buying with us. If we start to notice a pattern with customers who are not buying for similar reasons, we may need to change the way that we are dealing with things.

KNOW WHO YOUR COMPETITORS ARE

Running a business is tough. Consumers these days have so much choice and variety in product and price that you really need to stand out if they are going to buy from you. Look what your competition is doing, and then aim to constantly do better. You may not be able to always beat their prices, but you can definitely offer a higher quality of customer service than them – after all, sales businesses are built on relationships and repeat business.

BE PROFESSIONAL AT ALL TIMES

I'm Professional!

If your customer asks you a question that you don't know during your sales pitch, never make something up just to keep the pitch flowing. Tell your customer that you do not know, but you will find out the answer for them. You do not want to be caught out delivering false promises. Only talk about what you know, and maintain a high level of respect and professionalism with all of your customers at all times.

Chapter 6 – Cold Calling

Cold calling is the traditional practice of phoning unknown prospects in an attempt to establish business relationships with them. Whilst cold calling, you could be either selling your products or services, or simply setting up appointments with decision-makers who are responsible for making purchases. Over the years, cold callers, or telemarketers, have developed negative reputations and are considered to be nothing the sleazy salespeople who harass and intimidate people who do not want to buy, and the kind of salespeople who refuse to take no for an answer. However, cold calling is a legitimate form of marketing and is actually quite effective in developing long-lasting business and customer relationships just from a simple conversation over the phone.

WHAT DEFINES A COLD CALL

The definition of cold calling is simply the practice where a business or its sales representatives call potential customers to sell their products or services. It is called "cold" because the call is generally made without the prospects permission, and do not know the person calling them or the reason of the call. During the call, the sales representative will try and have a conversation with the prospect, normally from a script, in order to familiarize the customer with the business and its products.

WHAT MAKES A COLD CALL EFFECTIVE?

The effectiveness of a cold call is determined by a number of factors which will ultimately affect the outcome of the call. These factors include the personality of the sales representative (in this case, the telemarketer), how well they are able to use cold calling techniques, and how well they target the market which contains the prospects they would like as customers. Some studies have shown that you will close the deal, on average, 1 out of every 100 phone calls that you make, but this is not the attitude that you should have. Cold calling should not be considered a numbers game. If you look at it that way, out of every 100 customers that you call, 99 are going to be wasted, and only 1 will be worthwhile. You must consider **EVERY** call to be as important as the next, and you should be aiming to use all of the skills you have learned so far in this book in every call. There are successful telemarketers out there that have a success rate of up to 9 out of 10, so 90 sales out of every 100 phone calls. This should be your benchmark. Don't ever be discouraged however, just remember that every time that a customer says no, the next phone call could be a yes.

WHAT ARE SOME COLD CALLING TECHNIQUES?

Before you make a call, you should prepare, because in the telemarketing business, those who prepare will succeed. Not only should you know as much as possible about the products and services that you are selling, but you should also know everything about the brand or business that you are selling, who you target market is and why, and how you intend to actually go about having conversations with these prospects on the phone. The best technique when cold calling is to follow the sales strategy steps – ask the customer questions to identify their needs, listen to every word that the customer then says, asking for the sale and overcoming objections (the word "no"). Remember that you are trying to build relationships also, so if you put in the time and effort to reward your customer, your customer will reward you.

TOP TIPS OF SUCCESSFUL COLD CALLERS

You should be confident without coming across as cocky. This is achieved by making sure you listen to what the customer is saying and answer those questions without jumping in whilst they are talking to try and only close the deal as quick as possible. If you come across as genuinely confident, then it can be harder for customers to say no. People will listen to leaders and influential people, and this should go in par with your natural ability to be friendly and empathetic. Some of the most successful telemarketers and sales professionals say that when they pick up the phone, they smile whilst they are talking to the prospect or customer. This sounds silly since the customer cannot see you smiling through the phone, but believe it or not, you can hear people smiling through the phone – it comes across in the tone of your voice, and people will want to talk to people who are smiling.

You should also have a script which can guide you in your conversation on the phone. A script might be helpful when you first start out, but try and learn to have a conversation without it. Customers can hear if you are reading off of a script, because the conversation will become quite robotic and monotonous – and this will also give the customer the impression that it does not matter what they say to you, as you are not tailoring your answers to their problems to their specific needs, but rather only reading predetermined responses from a piece of paper.

On the note of research, although it may be near impossible to learn everything about a business or prospect before you call them (especially if you are calling individuals at their homes), you should still make sure that your research at least includes demographic research of your target market. For example, if you are selling your products or services to people who love skateboards, then research as much as you can about those people – what type of skateboards do they like, what brands do they prefer, what major factors will affect the type of skateboards that they purchase.

This rule can be applied to any target market. When you are having a conversation with a prospect over the phone, showing them that you are knowledgeable about the products that they love, then it will be much easier to develop relationships with them. It also helps you if they ask you a question about products in that market – you will have done your research so you should be able to answer them.

Most importantly however, you should be keeping good records of your calls and be taking notes from every call. Implement one of the sales tools that we looked at in a previous chapter to keep these records. That way, you will have a detailed list of people who you have called, have not called, objections, reasons for not buying, appointment times for call backs, and so on. You should also consider having a diary to keep a good record of dates and times that customers have requested you to call them back if they needed you to get more information or did not have the time to talk to you when you first called.

Conclusion

In summary, by reading this book you should now have the required basic skills to succeed in the sales industry. We have learned that sales is a personalized process which differs from marketing, and that successful salespeople share five traits – discipline, tenacity, implementation, focus, and desire. We have also learned that when we ask for the sale, we should be asking a question which makes the customer give a reason for why they are not going to buy today. This way, you can explore with the customer ways that you can overcome this objection.

This book has also shown you the various sales tools and sales strategies which will allow you to effectively develop your business into a very successful organization, and the key to this development is built upon developing long-lasting relationships with our customers by asking quality and relevant questions. Lastly, we looked at some simple cold calling techniques which you can use to increase your sales conversion rate when making phone calls to potential customers.

Use this book as a guide and reference on your journey to becoming a successful salesperson, and always remember that it is up to us to make the decision to be successful. Come back and read this book any time that you need to refresh your skills or need motivation or inspiration, as this book will surely help you succeed.

Thank you for reading. I hope you enjoy it. I ask you to leave your honest feedback.

14754360R00051

Printed in Great Britain
by Amazon.co.uk, Ltd.,
Marston Gate.